GLASS

HAMMER

POETRY BY ANDREW HUDGINS

Saints and Strangers (1985)
with an introduction by John Frederick Nims

After the Lost War: A Narrative (1988)

The Never-Ending: New Poems (1991)

The Glass Hammer: A Southern Childhood (1994)

THE GLASS HAMMER

A Southern Childhood

ANDREW HUDGINS

Houghton Mifflin Company
Boston New York

Library of Congress Cataloging-in-Publication Data

Hudgins, Andrew.
The glass hammer : a southern childhood / Andrew Hudgins.
p. cm.
ISBN 0-395-70011-6 (cl) ISBN 0-395-70010-8 (pbk)
1. Children — Southern States — Poetry. 2. Family — Southern States — Poetry. I. Title.
PS3558.U288G53 1994
811'.54 — dc20 93-43960
CIP

Printed in the United States of America

BP 10 9 8 7 6 5 4 3 2 1

Printed on recycled paper

Book design by Anne Chalmers

For my brothers

Let thine ear now be attentive, and thine eyes open, that thou mayest hear the prayer of thy servant, which I pray before thee now night and day, and confess the sins which we have sinned against thee: both I and my father's house have sinned.

— *Nehemiah* 1:6

In thoughts like these true wisdom may discern
Longings sublime, and aspirations high,
Which some are born with, but the most part learn
To plague themselves withal; they know not why:
'Twas strange that one so young should thus concern
His brain about the action of the sky;
If you think 'twas Philosophy that this did,
I can't help thinking puberty assisted.

— Byron, *Don Juan*

ACKNOWLEDGMENTS

Grateful acknowledgment is made to the following journals, in which some of the poems were first published:

The Atlantic: "Colonel," "Grandmother's Spit," "Haircut," "Thus"; *The Chronicle of Higher Education:* "The Benedictine Hand"; *The Colorado Review:* "Oh, Say, Can You See?" "Slap"; *The Elk River Review:* "Original Sin" (sections 2 and 5); *The Hudson Review:* "Acquired Taste," "Granny Raines," "My Father's Corpse," "My Father's Rage," "Original Sin" (sections 1 and 3); *The Kenyon Review:* "Salt," "Tree"; *The Massachusetts Review:* "Dangling"; *Michigan Quarterly Review:* "Blemishes"; *The New Criterion:* "Blue Tree," "Bright Leaf," "Dog Pile"; *The New England Review:* "Biff Burger," "Tricks of the Body," "Wisdom and Advice"; *The Paris Review:* "Aunt Mary Jean," "Fist," "Mother's Funeral," "The Visible Man"; *Ploughshares:* "After the Dance," "Teevee with Grandmomma," "Yellowjackets"; *Poetry:* "Burial Insurance"; *Princeton University Library Chronicle:* "Fireflies after Twilight"; *Salamander:* "Lists"; *Shenandoah:* "Begotten," "Gospel," "Patchwork," "The Telling," "Transistor Radio," "When I Was Saved"; *Southern Living:* "In a Car outside the Vineyard Baptist Church"; *The Southern Review:* "The Air," "Blue Danube," "Original Sin" (section 4), "Seventeen"; *Western Humanities Review:* "Childhood of the Ancients," "Mending Socks," "What a Grand World It Would Be!"

"When I Was Saved" was reprinted in *The Pushcart Prize XVII: Best of the Small Presses* (Wainscott, NY: Pushcart Press, 1992).

"Funeral Parlor Fan" and "Hunting with My Brother" were first published in *The Never-Ending* (Boston: Houghton Mifflin, 1991).

For fellowships and residencies that made possible much of the writing of this book I'd like to thank Yaddo, Ragdale, the Taft Foundation at the University of Cincinnati, and the National Endowment for the Arts. For comments on early versions of these poems I'm grateful to Christianne Balk, Jim Cummins, Randall Curb, John Drury, Mark Jarman, Walt Litz, Walt McDonald, Eric Pankey, Richard Selzer, Shawn Sturgeon, and Erin McGraw. Once again Peter Davison's editorial advice has been crucial. "James Bond Considers Career Opportunities in Library Science" is dedicated to Jim Cummins, and "Tree" is dedicated to Cheryl McKiearnan.

CONTENTS

II

III ❧

THE GLASS HAMMER

My mother's knickknack crystal hammer
shone on the shelf. "Put that thing down.
It's not a play-pretty." *Tap, tap,*
against my wooden blocks. "I said,
PUT THAT THING DOWN!"

But when she wasn't looking — ha! —
I'd sneak back to the hammer, and heft it.
Enchanted, I held it to my eyes
and watched, through it, the living room
shift, waver, and go shimmery — haloed

with hidden fire. Our worn green sofa glowed
and lost its shape, as if some deeper shape
were trying to break loose. The chairs,
the walls, the cross-stitched pictures all
let go, smeared into one another.

I scrounged a rust-flecked nail, and hit it.
The hammer shattered in my hand.
Blood spattered on my shorts. I screamed,
was snatched off my fat bloody feet,
rushed to the doctor, stitched, cooed at, spanked,

embraced, told *never, never, never*
do that again, and pondered how
I could, the hammer having burst,
and not, therefore, a proper hammer
despite the gorgeous world it held.

GRANNY RAINES

Inside the tilted shotgun shack, she waited:
one arm, one leg, one eye with a black patch.

Come here and hug old Granny Raines, she squawked.
Although just five, I knew what this was: witch.

Or close enough for me. "Go on!" Mom whispered,
shoved me. And Granny's blue eye glittered. She knew

she'd never see this boy again: great-grandchild,
her first. *Come to your Granny Raines*, she wheedled.

And when I sidestepped into reach, she grabbed me
and hugged my neck, pulled me into her scent

of mildew and Mentholatum. I gave myself to her.
Death seized Life, squeezed me, hugged me, kissed my lips.

ORIGINAL SIN

1

Taunted by older boys,
I'd run up, touch the tree
— a cedar white with droppings —
and hop back as the hens
pecked my pink ankles. Then
I'd lie awake at night
convinced I'd die: I'd watched
hens jab the dirty silk
of spider webs, jerk back,
pause, flip their heads, and swallow
live spiders. *Only a thing*
that's poisonous itself
eats spiders, Grandmomma said.
And I believed her. I'd seen them
rake each other's raw
red flaws until they'd crippled
or killed a bird that could
have been themselves. Or me.
But when Grandmomma marched
out to the tree, I followed
and crowed at the hens as she
grabbed one bird by the neck
and snapped her wrist. Waist-high,
held out away from her,
the dead bird walked on air
and flapped. I ran behind,

crowed, clucked, and flapped my arms
triumphantly, till Grandmomma
said, *Shush, boy,* and I shushed.

2

In noonday sun, the blue-
tailed skink's tail glittered a bright
metallic neon, and wanting it,
I reached and grabbed and fumbled
as the skink shot down the porch
rail, leapt, and flickered through
pine needles. But its tail,
a second reptile, squirmed
between my thumb and finger.
The skink grew a new blue whip,
but the one I'd stolen was
already lashing less
and less. I held it to the light
and studied it — each flicker,
each lessening of blue —
till it was motionless
and gray in my right hand
between my thumb and finger.

3

I cowered from the hens'
mean eyes and poison beaks.
Grandmomma'd snatch me back,
swat at the squawking hens,
palm their hot eggs, and cook
two fried-egg sandwiches.
I'd hold mine up before
my brother's face and squeeze
the unbroken yolk between
two slices of white bread.
It bulged. *Thump, thump!* I'd say.
Thump, thump! The tell-tale heart!
Thump, thump! It's coming to
get you! I clenched my fist
around the bread. The yolk
exploded. My brother screamed.
And I, before his face,
would eat the yellow heart.

4

Except for tennis shoes,
I was naked when I walked
back from the outhouse. A web
dissolved around my thighs,

and slapping at spiders that might
not even be there, I pitched
full length into the dirt
and rolled as if afflicted
because I'd seen, the year
before, my brother's hand
swell double from a brown
recluse's bite, his skin
so red and taut it glistened.
As boys, we'd caught small moths
and tossed them in a web.
The spider tiptoed up
while fierce wings ripped the frail
white-silk geometry.
They managed to tear loose
perhaps one time in three.
And though those strands were nothing
to my blundering, I leapt
into the dirt, clawing
at webs that might or might
not hold a poison mouth,
because I thought they should.

5

Two blocks away we heard
the fog truck whooshing toward
our street. In joy we dashed
from our half-eaten supper
to be transformed, to be
translated bodily
to idiot heaven. In the fog
we flailed, sang, shouted. Sharp edges
went soft and then dissolved.
And so did we. We ran,
blurring then taking form
before we blurred again,
invisible. The white
clouds tumbled down our street,
chased by enraptured children
who raced to stay inside
the thickest, most distorting clouds,
ecstatic in the poison.

BRIGHT LEAF

Some memories I've re-formed from photographs:
the tract house near Fort Hood, and the blue Dodge
I steered while Daddy drove. Some memories
I've scripted, blocked, and filmed from family stories:
Aunt Ruth says I'd crow "Androo fix!" and jab
my plastic wrench into the toaster. I loved
that yellow wrench. And once, apparently,
I talked Jack into eating fourteen pill bugs.
But this one I'd swear to on a hymnal:
I'm six. I'm hunkered by the state road, holding
a brown leaf fallen from a truck — tobacco,
cured brightleaf the color of the Constitution,
fragrant with red earth and perfumed with slow dying.
I held it to my face, experiencing
not rapture, transport, ecstasy, which I
have never known and don't expect to know,
but pleasure, which, with that leaf, I started learning.

MY FATHER'S CORPSE

He lay stone still, pretended to be dead.
My brothers and I, tiny, swarmed over him
like puppies. He wouldn't move. We tickled him,
tracing our fingers up and down his huge
misshapen feet — then armpits, belly, face.
He wouldn't move. We pushed small fingers up
inside his nostrils, wiggled them, and giggled.
He wouldn't move. We peeled his eyelids back,
stared in those motionless, blurred circles. Still,
he wouldn't, didn't move. Then we, alarmed,
poked, prodded his great body urgently.
Diddy, are you okay? Are you okay?
He didn't move. I reared back, gathered speed,
and slammed my forehead on his face. He rose,
he rose up roaring, scattered us from his body
and, as he raged, we sprawled at his feet — thrilled
to have the resurrected bastard back.

IN A CAR OUTSIDE THE VINEYARD BAPTIST CHURCH

I flipped the wings of my clip-on bow tie
up down, up down. *Sit still*, somebody hissed.
I wormed my finger down between my neck
and the hot collar, and slid it back and forth.
Calm down! Sit still! As we drove from the church
my mother's mouth worked soundlessly — a tool
that wouldn't catch, as when her Singer's bright
wild needle pounded on no cloth. Inside
that hot white church, I'd soon be born again.
My brothers too. But Da-daddy would not.
His births were finished, done. Not that I knew
one thing about his death or even why
we'd been in church this weekday afternoon.
Or why the house was full of casseroles
and somber strangers. A week from now I'd start
to wonder where Da-daddy was. I'd ask.
Momma would hug me, moan, try to explain.
But in the hot car, now, her bright red lips
churned wordlessly until they caught. She screamed.
My father, cousins, kin all say I'm wrong.
But that's how I remember it: she screamed.

SALT

As I dashed after sparrows, flinging
salt from the shaker, they hopped sideways
and hardly noticed me. My uncle shouted,
"Don't throw it — *sprinkle* it on their tails!"
I stalked them back and forth across
his yard and toward the highway, intent
on catching one, till I looked up and saw
my uncle, slack with laughter, leaning
against his truck. I didn't say *goddamn*
because I didn't possess the word —
or *fuck* or *shit* or *hell.* Instead,
enraptured by my rage, I reared back
and tossed his shaker high beyond scrub oak.
And Sonny stopped guffawing for one
moronically sweet moment before
his neck bulged and his face flared red.
He yelled, "You better find that thang!"
Which I did after nine that night,
by flashlight, in the hollow of a stump,
three-quarters hidden in stump water.

CHILDHOOD OF THE ANCIENTS

Hard? You don't know what hard is, boy:
When I was your age we got up in pitch dark,
and walked five miles to school and ten miles back,
uphill both ways, and all we had for lunch
was a cold sweet potato and dry cornbread.
And when we got back home your grandma made us
chop cotton, slop the hogs, then milk the chickens
before supper, and all we had to eat
was chicken-fried pine straw and redeye gravy.
Maybe some turnip greens. Maybe some collards.
But what do you know? Shoot, you've always had
hot food plopped in front of you, like magic.
For you, it's all ice cream and soda pop.

YELLOWJACKETS

Huge drowsy yellowjackets rose
out of the sick-sweet stink of fruit —
a tub of scuppernongs wedged in
between me and my uncle. He said,
"Hold that tub steady. Don't let her tip."
He drove and boasted of his new
air pump and how only fools would pay
full retail price. And when the wasps
bounced off his cheek, he flicked his wrist,
backhanded them toward me. I whimpered
and tried to burrow in the seat.
"Now hold her steady, boy. We don't
want all them grapes inside our shoes,
do we?"
"There's big wasps in the tub."
"Not wasps. They're yellowjackets. Look —
don't bother them and they won't bother you."
He warbled, "I'm a rambling wreck
from Georgia Tech," and nudged me to sing.
A yellowjacket smacked the windshield,
smacked the hot glass again, bounced back
and tangled in my hair. I screamed
and slapped at it. He stopped the truck.
I leapt out, batting at my hair,
my neck, shirt, face. He crushed me to him
while I fought back and sobbed. "There, there —
ain't you ashamed? A great big boy
like you — you little yellow thang."

Next day, I stood beneath barn eaves
and watched the yellowjackets pick
across the paper nest. I heaved
a dirt clod, stood still, got stung three times
— it seemed enough — before I ran.

Here's what I learned: first comes the jolt.
You think, It's going to hurt. Count one,
count two, not three: and then it comes,
the pain's oblivion, and you stop thinking.

Though grateful for that bit of knowledge,
I carried to the nest a cup
of kerosene, tossed it, and watched
the dead wasps tumble, backward, down.
The fire was just embellishment.
But I did, I embellished it.

GRANDMOTHER'S SPIT

To wipe the sleep grains from my eyes or rub
a food smudge from my cheek, Grandmother'd lick
her rough right thumb and order me, *Come here.*
She'd clutch my arm and hold me near her face
while, with that spit-damp thumb, she scrubbed the spot.
I struggled like a kitten being licked,
then leaned into the touch, again cat-like,
helping that fierce thumb scour loose the dirt.
It smelled, her spit, of lipstick and tobacco —
breath-warm, enveloping. She'd hold me at arm's length,
peer hard into my face, and state, *You're clean.*
When she let go, I'd crouch behind the door
and, with my own spit, rub the clean spot raw.

DOG PILE

Somebody'd yell, "Dog pile on Andrew!" I'd drop
my homework and tear across the asphalt,
trying to make it to the grass. Somebody
tackled me and slammed me to the hardtop.
I gasped as each late boy flopped on the pile
and jarred my breath loose. Under the pile,
I was a little bruised, a little angry,
a little pleased they knew my name, which is only
one of the dangers of a name. "Get off me!"
I bellowed, and flailed at the slow ones. My friends
peeled off the pile and waited for me to choose.
I paused dramatically, looked around, and yelled,
"Dog pile on Hudgins!" First everybody froze,
and then my brother started running.

AUNT MARY JEAN

As we stood by the casket, Momma gasped,
through tears, "Look hard. You must remember her!"
I looked hard, tried to memorize the slight
malicious curl of her thin lips — too red —
and then I studied how her dyed hair puffed,
blond around her pinched blond face. With powder,
the undertaker's hand was more restrained
than hers had been. And, all in all, I thought
she looked a little better dead — relaxed,
less mean, and more alive. Though not the way
that Momma meant, I've done what I was told:
remembered Mary Jean. It's Momma who's
becoming smudged and indistinct because
I've rubbed that memory featureless with grief.
But if she heard me call her Momma, "Boy,"
she'd snap, "I'm not your momma, I'm your mom."

WAS

It wasn't the big words that I lost
but the little piddly ones like *wuz*.
The harder I tried and the more
I sounded out the syllables,
the more mere music opened up
beneath my breath. The word, the world,
kept sliding. I raced downstairs and burst
into the kitchen. "Wuz, Momma, wuz!"
Puzzled, she stopped and stared at me.
"Wuz! How do you spell wuz?" She laughed.
"It's dub-ya, ay, ess. Okay, kiddo?"
The word clicked shut. I pressed my face
into her dark blue skirt and held her
until my breath slowed. "There, there —
they're only words on paper, Droops."
Drupes. Droopy-drawers. Androodles. Me.

HAIRCUT

"Quit sniveling! Sit still!" And in disgust
he palmed my head like a basketball
and forced it down and buzzed the clippers up
my neck again. Hair sifted down my collar.
I squirmed. He jerked the pink bath towel
tighter against my throat, and hair
flew up and landed in the sugar bowl.
Then gradually, to even out mistakes,
my hair grew shorter, more like stubble,
more like West Point or hot Fort Hood,
where I was born. We saved some money.
But now it's his turn and he sits,
hands folded on his lap, unsteady,
while I, with tiny scissors, snip
the gray hair curling from his nostrils
and from both ears; and, Jesus, at sixty
the death hairs really get their growth,
don't they? The scissors pinch his skin
and he tries not to flinch. "Sit still!"
I snarl, and I'm so horrified
I say it one more time. "Sit still."

THREATS AND LAMENTATIONS

I'll jerk a knot in your tail, boy.
Jack's staring at me. He's touching me.
Mom, George is breathing on my face.
What *am* I going to do with you?
Go shake the dew off your lily.
We won't be stopping every five yards
for you to pee. Don't try me, boy.
Shut up or I'll blister your behind.
I'll slap you silly. I'll tan your bottom.
No one can love you like I do.
Mom, Andrew spit in my Kool-Aid.
You'll be the death of me. If you
don't pull that pouty lip back in,
I'll knock it back in place for you,
young man. Just once I'd like to pee
without somebody yelling "Mom!"
Mom, Andrew's breathing on my pillow.
Each night I pray for you. You hush now.

THE TELLING

Dawn overtook Scheherazade and she fell silent.
"Hey, Mister Antisocial, Mister Unconscious —
come join the family," Mom called. Ignored her.
"Nerd, nerd, nerd is the word," my uncle sang.
Fuck him. It's night again. Scheherazade
tells of the fisherman who caught four fish:
one red, one blue, one white, one yellow. He's puzzled.
The demon says, Take them to the caliph.
And I decided, yes, that's good enough:
she gets to live another day. I flipped
the pages eagerly. What next? What next?
And, lucky Andrew, Baptist boy, he read,
he made the trip to Mecca, he met the caliph.

FUNERAL PARLOR FAN

Inside the Vineyard Baptist Church,
the funeral parlor fans — tick tock —
snapped the hot air in the faces of
grandmother, mother, aunt. They kept
a steady out-of-sequence beat.
They never faltered. Me, I faltered.
I'd lay the creased fan on my lap
and stare at Jesus kneeling in
Gethsemane. He didn't look
like someone pleading not to die.
If I were him, I'd blubber worse
than when my daddy snapped his belt
out backward, popping through the loops,
tick tock. With a child's cunning, I screamed
before that thin strap stung my thighs.
This Jesus didn't seem to get it: men
were going to drive three nails through him
and into wood and let him hang
there, writhing, till he died. I shuddered.
But I was eight and there were lots
of things I didn't get. I fanned
a little more, grew bored, and jabbed
my brother, kicked the seat in front of me
till, casually, my mother's hand
dipped out and popped my head, not hard,
with Jesus praying in the garden
or, flipped, Hobb's Funeral Home. And just
to hear myself talk, I'd say *ouch*

and get another dose of Jesus,
and slightly harder too. The beat
resumed: tick tock, tick tock, and I
took up the worn, two-sided fan
and tried — small hands — to keep the beat.
Tick: Jesus. Tock: Hobb's Funeral Home.

ACQUIRED TASTE

Sprawled on my Roy Rogers bedspread,
book on the floor, head down, I read
of Long John Silver, buried gold —
and as I read I worked a penny
between my thumb and Daddy's metal file.
And when it dwindled thin enough,
I scraped the edges and increased
my holdings one thousand percent
so I could, once a week, entice
a soda from the box. Time after time,
I pitched my false dime through the slot
before I heard the slow *ka-chunk*
and the red box disgorged a stolen Coke
that detonated in my mouth,
and stung. Cold needles pricked my tongue.
I took another painful swallow,
not liking or desiring it,
but wanting to, desiring that,
and penny, penny, penny — dime,
dime, dime — I kept on till I did.

TRANSISTOR RADIO

Summer nights I huddled under
bedsheets in the hot dark
of my own breathing, ear pressed
against my father's radio.
This was forbidden: listening
to songs of cheating lovers,
lost unrecovered loves,
drink, song itself, and making
believe. I yearned and feared
to suffer that suffering
so the hurt would justify
my pure unhappiness,
at last. And now we march,
conscripts of sorrow who first
were volunteers. I hummed,
ignorant of what it meant:
walking the floor, you've got
that faraway look
in your eyes. But knowing that
I would find out, I sang
the forbidden words, ears pressed
to older worlds, in the hot
dark of my own slow breathing.

FIREFLIES AFTER TWILIGHT

The intermittent flick of light so quick
I wasn't sure it was a light
but something my drowsy eye had tricked
out of its fear of darkness, which
pressed into the screened-in porch
where I lay watching, afraid, but not enough
to move back in the house, which sweltered:
the fireflies rose. Rarely more
than one light quavered at a time,
flicking its diminishing sexual light
against the crowded pines. Eros
and Thanatos I'll call it now,
but then I simply called it fear.
If I'm still frightened — and I am —
it's complicated with yearnings
toward doubleness and indecision:
how during sunlight I block light,
which warms my back and loosens me,
while after dark I stand out, white
against the black pines — usually
but not always at odds with nature,
God and the gods, whom I resisted
when I crushed fireflies on my cheeks,
a war paint of false light, then dashed
from moonbeam to tree shadow, stalking. . .
Not stalking anything, just stalking
till I was sleepy. The fireflies rise until

it's been a long time with no light
against the darkness. I'm gone, I'm nothing,
and then it's sunrise, morning, day.

II

BEGOTTEN

I've never, as some children do,
looked at my folks and thought, I *must*
have come from someone else —
rich parents who'd misplaced me, but
who would, as in a myth or novel,
return and claim me. Hell, no. I saw
my face in cousins' faces, heard
my voice in their high drawls. And Sundays,
after the dinner plates were cleared,
I lingered, elbow propped on red
oilcloth, and studied great-uncles, aunts,
and cousins new to me. They squirmed.
I stared till I discerned the features
they'd gotten from the family larder:
eyes, nose, lips, hair? I stared until,
uncomfortable, they'd snap, "Hey, boy —
what are you looking at? At me?"
"No, sir," I'd lie. "No, ma'am." I'd count ten
and then continue staring at them.
I never had to ask, What am I?
I stared at my blood-kin, and thought,
So *this*, dear God, is what I am.

TEEVEE WITH GRANDMOMMA

The blue light of the teevee glowed
on our blue faces. Ray Charles sang
of Georgia on his mind. “His mind?
That nigger doesn’t have a mind,”
Grandmomma said. She threw her tatting
on her lap, sighed, glowered at the set.
“Damn niggers taking over teevee. You can’t
watch Johnny Carson anymore
for all the niggers.”
                    “Now Momma, hush
that kind of talk in front of the boys,”
my mother said. And I chirped up,
“They’re just like us, you know. At school
my teacher says that colored people
are just like us.”
                    “Well, maybe they’re
like you,” she growled, and glared at me
to see what I’d say. Long pause. Then I,
to make her angrier, agreed.

WHAT A GRAND WORLD IT WOULD BE!

Between us, Miz Porter tapped her yardstick hard
against the floor. "All right now, class, let's see
which side can sing louder today. Girls first."

I wish the boys were all transported FAR
beyond the Northern Sea! "That isn't loud,"
she chided. "Now, boys, you sing." She pointed at us.

I WISH the GIRLS were ALL transPORted FAR
beyond the Northern Sea! "Now louder, girls! —
Now boys!" We banged the rhythm on our thighs.

We stomped the floor. Neck muscles bulged.
And I came close to fainting and fell silent.
I only mouthed the words. Across the room

the girls looked just as lunatic as us.
Eyes fixed, hair snapping back and forth,
the breastless girls snarled at soprano boys.

The split refrains merged, stumbled, crashed to silence,
and we glared at each other's otherness
over the empty desks. And in the gulf

Miz Porter kept on shouting, "Louder, louder!"

THE VISIBLE MAN

Grandmomma plucked pinfeathers. I stared
into the cavity and tried
to imagine such jumbled meaty things
inside my belly. She saved the liver
and tossed the heart aside. "How come?"
"The Bible says don't eat a heart."
But when she wasn't watching me
I snatched it from the sink and ate it,
unnoticed, as if I were invisible.
When, younger, I stared at the burners,
Momma would say, "Uh-uh, don't touch."
I gawked. How had she read my mind?
"Your life's an open book to me,
young man." It made me wild. I'd yell,
pout, kick the kitchen cabinet, sulk.
I wanted to be subtle. Well, subtle
and just a bit malicious. I longed
to waft among my family, the world,
like Casper the not-so-friendly ghost,
unseen. It didn't work. When I passed
the teevee, Mom said, "Sit down.
You make a better door than a window."
I longed to be a window. Inside
The Visible Man's invisible shell,
I'd glued the heart, lungs, kidneys, liver.
But inside me? I had my doubts.
Mom said, Snips, snails, and puppy tails.
Then piss and vinegar. Then meanness,
pure meanness. I liked the dignity of that.

BLEMISHES

Head tilted back in Mom's lap,
a warm damp washrag on my face,
I blabbed about whatever book
I'd fallen for that evening: *Penrod*
or *Seven Days in May.* She lifted
the lukewarm rag and popped my zits
between her red thumbnails. "Hey, Mom —
am I good looking?" She thought about it,
and, upside down, she looked me over.
"Your face has lots of character."
She paused, considered, let it stand.
It wasn't a surprise. At school
they called me Pudgins and Nigger Lips,
so character was a lie more thoughtful
than I had bargained for. Mom squeezed.
Ouch! "Hush. Now that one really popped."
She oohed over how much it oozed
and held the pus up on her thumbnail
and showed it to me. I oohed too.
"Good night, sweet prince," she said, and laughed
and dropped the cool rag on my face.

BLUE DANUBE

As we clung to the corner and catcalled,
Miz Caldwell waltzed her tall befuddled friend
across the room. When the record circled past
the last note, she twirled her partner to a halt.
The needle scraped. Miz Caldwell turned to us
and said, "A waltz — that's how it's done. You try!
One-two-three, one-two-three." And by her side
the taller woman blinked, swayed sleepily,
as if she'd just awakened. "Don't count steps. Glide!"
We tangled in our box steps, frustrated, and she,
frustrated too, shrieked, "No, no, no! This way!"
She locked her palm against her partner's back
and drove her hard across the floor, bent backward
in cha-cha-chas or held elegantly
erect in waltzes, so dedicated to the dance
she wouldn't stop and break it into steps
for us to follow. She didn't care. They danced,
and went somewhere we couldn't go, and left us
shuffling in the rec room of First Methodist,
flat-footed, untransported. Across their feet
we slithered pennies, nickels, and even dimes.
They didn't miss a step. The needle rose.
She pushed it down again — "Blue Danube" — and smiled,
smiled tightly. "You boys! Let's see what you have learned."

SKEETER KITES

We paid out black thread pilfered from the mill.
It curved up toward our kites. Unsteady, swooping,
they dipped, cut zeros in erratic air,
before they righted and rose out of sight.
When the stolen thread went slack, slid backward, looping
across loblolly pines, we snapped it off and jabbed
more dry stalks through more pages of *The Gleam*
and fed them to the currents over us. We laughed,
insulted one another's coats and ties,
even the coats and ties of Uncle Sonny's boys,
though Sonny'd be buried in an hour or two.
But now, the black thread tugging at our hands,
kites skittering, we had forgotten Sonny.
The grown-ups knew. They'd taken us outside,
away from the weeping and long silences,
and shown us how to make the skeeter kites
because they understood how Uncle Sonny
had drifted, and broken free of us. I didn't.
And I have learned to misdoubt metaphor,
its flimsy sticks, used paper, stolen thread.

LISTS

At twelve I wrote wills. I'd bequeath
my Bible to Daddy, my book of leaves
to Momma, who'd gathered and taped them
in last year's phone book. Sometimes
I'd leave my baseball cards and comics
to the boy who lived next door. He praised
the pleasures of a stump-trained heifer
and bragged of clubbing someone's goat to death.
But you don't really want to know.
I did. Eros and Thanatos —
I couldn't guess what they were, where
they'd lead me, when they'd raise their voices,
how beautifully or raucously
they'd sing, if sing was what they'd do.
Instead, I held to things that I
could touch, hold, read, list, count, and study,
although I knew that they weren't much
and wouldn't last till morning. The list
of what I'd take with me was short:
my soul. It was my daddy's answer:
an entity beyond belief against
a fate I couldn't comprehend.
That's how I lived much of my life:
afraid, and loving things because
I hadn't had enough of them; in love
with women who have loved me first;
and longing for a larger story
because my story overflowed with lists:

the Bible's endless *begats,* of which
Daddy never skipped a one;
birch, dogwood, cedar, sassafras;
and the hard constant work of memory.
Fig, red oak, plum. The house of David.

GOSPEL

"Jesus will always be there. He's waiting. It's true."
He wiped his forehead, crooned, began to sway:
"Softly and tenderly Jesus is calling you.

O sinner, come home. Come start your life anew.
I'll stand here as the organ gently plays.
Jesus will always be there. He's waiting. It's true."

I squirmed and giggled in the farthest pew,
then jabbed my best friend, smirked. He wouldn't play.
"Softly and tenderly Jesus is calling you."

Too soft for me. I picked dirt off my shoe.
I drummed my fingers and watched my best friend pray.
"Jesus will always be there. He's waiting. It's true."

Well, let him wait, I thought. He's overdue.
We get home after kickoff every Sunday.
"Softly and tenderly Jesus is calling you."

I prayed the preacher'd save a soul or two
so he'd shut up and let me go. He swayed.
Jesus is always there. He's waiting. It's true.
Softly and tenderly Jesus is calling you.

TRICKS OF THE BODY

I'd lunge from behind doors, and bellow.
You'll be the death of me, Mom sighed.
But once, Grandmomma, startled, spat
her yellow dentures from her mouth,
then caught them in midair, one-handed,
as if it were a trick she'd practiced.
And we both howled. But years before
I'd peeped around the door and seen
Grandmomma reach into her mouth and slip
her false teeth past her lips. I gagged
and retched while, in the jar, white bubbles
exploded upward. The teeth, in their
penultimate removal, bleached —
the half-grin grinning at its unclean half.

TREE

I'd like to be a tree. My father clinked
his fork down on his plate and stared at me.
"Boy, sometimes you say the dumbest things."
You ought to know, I muttered, and got backhanded
out of my chair. Nowdays, when I chop wood
and my hands gum with resin and bark flakes,
I hunker at the tap and wash them human.
But in math class, I'd daydream of my choices:
not hickory or cedar, not an oak —
post, red, live, pin, or water oak. Just pine.
If not longleaf, I'd settle for loblolly.
My skin would thicken with harsh bark, my limbs
sprout twigs, my twigs sprout elegant green needles.
Too soon, Miz Gorrie'd call on me. "Why did
you do step four that way?" *Who me? Step four?*
"Yes, Andrew, you. Step four." *Beats me. It looked
good at the time, I guess* — and got invited
to come back after school and guess again.
And that's when I decided it: scrub pine.

THE AIR

Because I'd seen a man
thrust his straight fingers through
a melon, I spent childhood
stalking a long hall, punching
the air in front of me.
Punch where your throat would be!
Kick where your crotch would be!
the sensei yelled. I grunted,
screamed fiercely, and snapped my fists,
driving them through the soft parts
of the me that wasn't there.
I punched pure air and tried
to shatter it — the air,
which simply opened, fell back,
gave way as my hands slashed through.
The air! I can't believe
how much I hated it.

PATCHWORK

From the scrap barrel at work I pilfered scraps —
rags, ends of bolts. Grandmomma jerked
thread through the cloth so hard the batting bulged.
We fought for those crude quilts, me and my brothers.
She yanked the stitches till they puckered, and slowly
the stolen scraps yielded a Drunkard's Path.

Grandmomma's ten years dead and her bad work
still keeps me hot at night, in Northern weather,
which she despised, just as she hated you
if you were Northern, rich, black, smart, or atheist.
I loved her because, like God, she loved me first,
ferociously. A love so close to hate
it's taken decades just to say there is a difference.

I sat between her knees, head tilted back.
She thumbed the crusty threads. "There ain't no call
paying some doctor to do this." She snipped
the threads lacing my forehead, popped them out.
But first she studied them and said, "It's sloppy —
these big loose stitches. I'd sew you tighter." She grinned,
and with a lipless peck she kissed the stitches.

BLUE TREE

We slipped the branches from wax-paper sheaths
and jabbed them on the shaft. A color wheel
lit tinsel branches red, blue, green, and yellow
until one year it stuck and yellow melted.
From the crawl space other trappings emerged:
the box of used and reused Christmas bows
and wrapping paper bought last January.
And after everything was up, ablaze,
I'd slip into the living room and survey
the presents, which I had poked and picked at and,
when necessary, unwrapped and rewrapped.
I knew them all. They never seemed enough.
Even the lavish piles in storybooks
seemed paltry, limited, compared to what
I could imagine getting. Bright colors spun
across the tinsel branches until, at last,
I wondered what they meant, the changing colors.
Green, sure, for summer. Red for fall, and yellow
for those last clinging leaves before the limbs
blow empty. But blue, what did blue mean?
It meant blue snow. It meant the twilight sky,
death, dreams, impossibility, or sorrow.
I hefted each thought, shook it, peeled it open.
Each meaning did its song and dance. Each meaning
put on its little dog-and-pony show.
I taped them, set them by the tree for later.
The color wheel churned round again: blue tree.

FIST

My daddy slapped my hand against my cheek.
"Don't hit yourself. Why are you hitting yourself?"
He held my wrists. I cried and wrestled. My hands,
completely out of my control, slapped me.
And then I did it to my brother, whom God,
in his great wisdom, delivered unto me
each time my parents left the house. With glee,
I'd smack his pink face till he begged,
and then a little longer.

Fourteen or so,
I wondered how I'd take a punch if some
drunk in a bar demeaned me or my woman.
I'd stand before the mirror, cock my fist,
and drive an uppercut into my cheek.
"Not good enough," I said. "You flinched."
I crawled up off the floor and tried again.

MAGIC BUTTON

My uncle gouged a circle in the dirt,
then closed the knife against his thigh. “See that?
Let’s say that circle there’s a magic button.
Let’s say nobody’d see you if you pressed it,
nobody’d ever know. But if you did,
the niggers all would disappear, like *that.*”
He snapped his fingers.
                                        “But that’s murder!” I said.
“Nope. They wouldn’t die. They’d disappear.
And all their nigger shit would go with them —
loud music, dope, and welfare.” I tried again:
“Come on! It isn’t like they stood in line
to ride those wonderful slave ships.”
                                                    “I know
how they got here. That’s not what I’m discussing.
I’m only asking whether you’d press the button
if nobody’d know, nobody’d see. I would,”
he said, and ground his bootheel on the circle.
We stood there a long time, not talking, staring
at the deep circle cut into the dirt.

In Thomas Jefferson’s first memory
a slave transports him on a silken pillow.

SIT STILL

The preacher said, "We know God's word is true."
Amen, somebody called. "How do we know?
We know because the Bible says it's true."
He waved the fraying book. "God says it's true.
And, brother, that's good enough for me." *Amen!*
My father's eyes were calm, my mother's face
composed. I craned around, but everyone
seemed rapt as Brother Vernon spun
tight circles of illogic. A change
that I could not resist swept through,
and I resisted it. I tried again
to sing the word behind the words we sang.
I prayed. Then I gave up and picked a scab
till Daddy popped my thigh and hissed, "Sit still."
Up front, the preacher waved his thick black book.
He fanned the pages, smacked it with his palm,
and I sincerely wished that I were stupid.

THE BENEDICTINE HAND

"Now class," she said, "we must be careful when
we push the glass tube through the stopper, thus."
She slid it halfway through the rubber hole.
It stuck. She rammed it harder, twisted. It snapped,
and, snapping, drove the ragged end of glass
into her palm. Blood dribbled on the desk.

"Now that's what you are not supposed to do,"
she said. She held two frozen fingers up,
as if to bless us. "I've cut the median nerve.
This is what's called the Benedictine Hand.
It's paralyzed." She flexed her thumb and last
two fingers. The blessing fingers stayed erect.
Then, pale, she wrapped her red hand in a wad
of towels, left the room — quick, angry steps.

We boys, although it wasn't accurate,
thereafter called her Mrs. Claw, not telling
each other how we squirmed that day or how,
dear Mrs. Claw, we won't forget the bright
blood, Benedictine Hand, or with what steel
you held before us your new deformity,
named it, explained it, and blessed us with your error.

THUS

Before I went to bed, I'd show
my father what I'd done that night.
The work was always smudged. I'd strain
to set the problem up, then beat
the numbers into it. Hunched
over the kitchen table, I'd copy
each page until he said it looked
acceptable. *Quit sniffling,* he'd say.
I'll give you something real
to cry about. And he was right.
I knew, even then, I wasn't entitled
to misery. My father'd put his head
down close to mine and say,
softly, *You've never had to worry*
where your next meal is coming from.
What could I say? From algebra
I was learning Plato — nothing fancy —
learning that numbers were more cruel
than I could ever hope to be,
and I had hoped to be ruthless.

SWING BLADE

Toad, field mouse, rabbit, bobwhite leapt
before my blade. With every swing
the weeds collapsed in thick, wet hanks.
Slick hickory slipped through my pink hands,
and for the blistering I learned
work could be swapped for money. At the end
of that long August afternoon,
I panted and watched as a neighbor
counted three quarters, cold and heavy
as individual cubes of ice,
on my raw palm. I jammed them in my pocket
and jiggled them for days, for weeks.
"They're burning a hole in your pocket,"
Mom laughed. Dad too. But they were wrong.
I couldn't trade the work away
so easily, so soon. Besides,
one quarter of the three was stamped
(and cupped with the force of stamping): *Bob
loves Donna.* I wanted to preserve
whatever Bob and Donna once
had cherished. Then, when that passed, I wanted
to honor what they'd put aside —
spent passion. That too passed. My blisters healed.
The cut grass bleached yellow in the ditch.
I cut it twice more, blistered once,
and after a while, like Bob or Donna,
I spent the quarters carelessly
on a paperback or Hershey bars

because sometimes — not all the time —
that's how you have to live your life.
Careful, careful, mince, mince, mince —
I'd had too much of that already.

SLAP

She slammed into the room,
threw on the light, yelled, "See!
See what your father did!"
Eyes dazzled, half asleep,
we didn't see a thing.
She shoved her cheek, blazed red,
into our faces. She yelled
till we said yes, we saw.
With that she started sobbing
and Daddy timidly
led her to bed. Two days
passed from our lives before
he came to each of us,
each boy, sat facing him,
and made himself say *sorry*,
say *shame*, say *love*. Embarrassed,
I held back, watched his throat
trembling and choking with crude
abstractions; then I rushed
to forgive him so he'd just
stop talking, talking. This time
he hadn't done a thing
to me. She had. It's her
I wanted to forgive.

WHEN I WAS SAVED

"Do you still have a demon in your heart?"
the preacher asked. I did. My heart
and some place lower too. The demon kicked
inside my body, heart and groin — the way
I'd felt my brother kick inside my mother.
The demon too was blood-kin. In my aisle seat,
I sweated and I had no doubt — still don't —
that Satan owned my heart. In tears,
I staggered down the aisle and, blubbering,
was saved. A prayer. A hymn. More tears. And then
the preacher led me like a trophy back
up that long aisle. My father, radiant,
stepped out and bear-hugged me so hard I gasped.
Later that day I couldn't breathe at all
when I, damp handkerchief clamped on my mouth,
was lowered into death. I went down easy,
stayed, panicked, struggled, and was yanked back up,
red-faced and dripping. After that, each Sunday
I went to preaching early so I could sit
behind a boy whose torn right ear did not
attach entirely to his head. Through that
pink gap of gristle, I'd watch the preacher shout,
croon, soothe — between that boy's head and his ear.
More sinners lumbered up the aisle. I longed
to run up and again be purged of Adam,
who was reborn each night, like Lazarus,
by my own hand, beneath the sweat-drenched sheets.

MY FATHER'S RAGE

As I kicked through the swinging door,
the turkey shifted on the platter.
I juggled, lost it, clipped the bird
with the platter's edge, and the hot meat
slid, skittered — greasy — on the floor,
and smacked the polished army boots
of Sergeant Walker, our Thanksgiving guest.
My daddy grabbed me by the throat
and slammed me up against the wall,
which boomed. My mother gasped. I lost
my breath and couldn't get it back.
"You stupid idiot!" my father screamed.
Then Sergeant Walker touched Dad's arm.
"John," he said, "we've eaten worse —
when we were growing up." Dad sighed,
and then, reluctantly, he let me drop.
But now his crazy anger's gone
to whole days watching teevee, watching
golf, football, weather — gone to whole days
watching the fucking all-news channel.
And I, goddamn him, I want it back.

III

I was still the same,
Knowing myself yet being someone other
— "Little Gidding"

SIDNEY LANIER HIGH

Look at those titties! Man, if she had
as many peckers sticking out
as she'd had stuck in her, she'd look
like a porcupine. Shit, no — not cheese grits!
Explain step four again please, Andrew.
I think you'll find a problem there.
4-H: One of them rabbits bit me,
so I picked up some garden shears
and held 'em by the scruff and knifed 'em,
all of the bastards. Math: There's no
such thing as an imperfect rose.
You tell and I'll beat you to death.
Coach Tinsley talked about anything
but government, which he was teaching:
They lifted it with a car jack,
then grabbed the nigger's feet and spun him.
His legs came free but his head swung under
just as the jack let go. The truck
exploded his head like a melon. Twelve
cheerleaders called, "Who are the poets?"
We shouted back, *We are the poets!*
"What kind of poets?" *Fighting poets!*
One pep-squad goober pinned huge pom-poms
over his clothes. From the front row,
a football player snapped a match
and Mister Pom-pom went up in flames.
They dedicated the yearbook to him.
And Mrs. Constable explained,
The Yankees stole the family silver.
That's why we're so poor in the South.

JAMES BOND CONSIDERS CAREER OPPORTUNITIES IN LIBRARY SCIENCE

Christ was a carpenter and Paul made tents.
Since all I really cared to do was read,
Dad drove me to the downtown library. For free,
I shelved books and learned what I already knew:
I didn't want to spend my life unearthing
lost novels, census reports, and recipes.
I shoved a chair into the history stacks
and read James Bond, which I was not allowed
to read at home. I brooded about packing
a Colt or a Beretta, and of the girls,
I'd choose not Pussy Galore but Domino.
Poor Daddy didn't know what to do with me.
I wanted to be stirred, not shaken — whatever that meant.

JACK

"I've got to pee." "I'm hungry." "I want to stop."
And Daddy jerked the car onto the shoulder.
"You want to get out? Okay, then – get out!"
We did, and he drove slowly out of sight,
watching the mirror. I started blubbering

but Jack just said, "Let's go." We marched,
and gravel crunched beneath our feet
till Daddy, laughing, roared back up. He laughed
at me for being so relieved, at Jack's
pretending not to care. But that was Jack.

When Daddy snapped his belt off, I started screaming.
Not Jack. We'd kneel across the sofa, butts
raised in the air, our pants around our ankles,
and while I bellowed, Jack gritted his teeth
and made no sound except the grunt or two

knocked out of him so Daddy couldn't say
"You're not hurt, you just think you are."
When we were small, I'd knock Jack to the ground
and kick him in the belly. He'd curl
around my foot and moan and, Jesus, I thought

I'd ruptured him. I'd crouch beside his head
and beg him not to tell. But he kept growing.
When Daddy laced us into boxing gloves

and shoved us at each other, I couldn't block
his hard, quick hands. I tried to cover up,

and Daddy, disgusted, smacked me to the ground.
This fighting business wasn't working out.
Last fight: Mom stepped between us as we yelled.
I reached around her head and popped him in the mouth.
"Please let me at him! Please!" he sobbed, and tried

to slide past Mom without touching her,
and I, sidestepping to keep her body between us,
yelled, "Come on. Yeah, come on, Mister Big Mouth!"
"You're brothers. You're supposed to love each other,"
Mom wailed. "Yeah, sure. On the Pollyanna planet."

I hoped I looked as crazy as he did,
hands snatching past her shoulders, grabbing for me,
till I pushed Mom aside, kicked at his balls,
missed, fought as best I could, and took my beating.

MENDING SOCKS

Late. Dad asleep and Johnny Carson on.
Perched on a child's cane-bottomed rocker, Mom
darned socks, sipped watered Scotch from a juice glass,
and laughed at Johnny's jokes. And then she talked.
Which uncles drank and where they hid the bottle.
Which cousin lost a child or had to marry.
Another sip. Her voice grew still more hushed.
She talked about her brother Little Pete,
who died at five — about her sister's boy,
a child who didn't seem right in the head.
Then Johnny'd crack a joke about L.A.
She'd pause and listen, laugh, repeat the joke,
and laugh again. A sip. Then suddenly
she'd glare at me and hiss, "It's family.
It stays in these four walls." I'd say, "Yes, ma'am,"
and she'd hand me a pile of mended socks.
I hated them — the knot of bunched-up thread
that ground into my instep and made me limp.
Soon as I turned the corner, I'd peel them off
and walk to school bare-ankled, which was the fashion.

OH, SAY, CAN YOU SEE?

"Granddaddy owned half of Marengo County,"
she said. First date. Last date. "Wow, half the county!"
I said. But what I thought was this:
Right now your daddy sells appliances,
your mom's a keypunch operator. My dad?
"He's in the service." She reeled off a list
of generals, heroes, governors — the assorted
effluvium of Southern history whom
she had descended from. Well, whup-dee-do.

I stood beside Dad's chair. "Who are we kin to?"
I asked. The blue light flickered.
Herman and Lily Munster mugged and snuggled.
Dad looked a little helpless. So I pressed:
"You know — rich people, politicians, famous thieves."
The Munsters, in their blue world, discovered Grandpa
hanging from an attic rafter, upside down.
"I've heard we're kin to Francis Scott Key." Don't ask,
they say, if you don't want to know.
Since then I've pondered blood
a quarter of a century off and on
and I find it hard to give a shit. Mom, Dad,
and two grandmommas were all it took
to get me born and teach me how to read
and how to hold a fork. More than enough,
my well-bred darlings, more than uh-fucking-nuff.

WISDOM AND ADVICE

Sit straight and don't slouch. Don't whine.
No matter how poor you are, you can
always be clean. Burp, fart, and hiccup
at the same time and it'll kill you.
"I can't" never did nothing. *My uncle:*
A blue-gum nigger'll cut your heart out.
When I repeated it, my father
grabbed, held me by my bunched shirtfront:
"Nobody wants to hear that word.
Nobody!" You'll eat what's put before you.
Mom: You can trust your Aunt Sue
just like she was blood-kin. Don't mumble.
The preacher: If the world was perfect,
we wouldn't have to love it. *Uncle:*
When people start to spill their drinks,
go home. *Another uncle:* At twenty
all I could think about was pussy.
At forty all I could think about
was money. I'm sixty now and all
I think about is one good shit.
First uncle, before my wedding: "Put up
with more shit than you ever thought you would.
When things get really bad, eat something.
That seems to help." Sit straight. Don't mumble.
The world's not made to make you happy.
So put that in your smoke and pipe it.

BIFF BURGER

I jerked Cokes. At fourteen it
seemed complicated: the flimsy cups,
the exact quantity of ice,
the cola foaming to the brim,
not over. Ninety cents an hour
and working for a boss who grinned
and winked while watering
the soft-drink syrup. One waitress offered
to claw my fucking eyeballs out.
I'm not sure why. The grill man draped
a tattooed forearm on my shoulder.
"Don't ever hit your daddy," he said,
and I said gravely that I wouldn't.
Tears trickled down his face. I liked
the empty syrup jugs because
I'd hook a finger through each thick
glass handle and, inside the dumpster,
I'd swing glass against glass. One day
the boss saw blood drip down my neck
and made me stop. Fuck him. I'd sooner
have stayed at home and read *Hawaii,*
The Fountainhead, and *Exodus.* Instead,
I jerked Cokes, scraped the grill. I drained
the hot fat, hosed the dumpster, swept.
And once while I was swabbing it,
the ice machine short-circuited.
My muscles jerked shut and I flew
across the back room backward and slammed
against the wall. First job: the sense
of being airborne violently.

THE RAPTURE

The dead in Christ shall rise first: then we which are alive and remain shall be caught up together with them in the clouds.

1 Thessalonians 4:16–17

I was a slack-jawed moron, credulous,
almost a cretin. They got me to chase sparrows
with a salt shaker in my hand. They told me
the moon was made of cheese and the tooth fairy
had only dimes left when she got to us.
I knelt astride paths, holding a croker sack
for snipes to run into. But even I
did not believe the dead, restored to flesh,
would hurtle from their graves. And after them
the living saints, zapped in midbreath, would blast
into the sky like bottle rockets.
But I imagined doing what I did
when everybody left the house. I'd crank
Mick Jagger on the stereo so loud
the music cracked. I screamed along. My voice,
lost in the raw distorted clamor, soared,
the last voice in the whole abandoned world —
or so it seemed, till Mom's car door slammed shut.

AFTER THE DANCE

We pulled into her driveway, kissed teevee style:
no tongues. Oh, twice or so I bumped my tongue
against her clenched teeth. No go. She pulled away,
curled a loose strand of hair behind her ear
and patted it. Then nervously she asked,
"At your house when you spill your milk or something,
does your mom make you suck it off the table?"
"Hell, no!" I said. Then, catching on: "Does yours?"

At home, in the dark kitchen, I dribbled milk
across the counter, slurped it up, and jumped
and almost choked when Mother hit the light.
"What *are* you doing?" I stood and stared at her,
stood searching for a lie — the ring of milk
ghost-white and undeniable on my lips.
"I spilled some milk." She shook her head, amused
and baffled, but not as baffled as I was
when I sat primly on her deathbed, transfixed
by the white crust of Maalox on her mouth.
But in the moment's innocence, she said,
"Kiss me good night." I did, and with a laugh
she wiped my white lips with her sleeve, then hers.

COLONEL

My father lifts the crippled airman's body
and jokes about how light he is and how
we need some rain. He holds him while the man's
young wife strips off the yellowed linen, cracks
white sheets above the bed and lets them drift
across the mattress. She smooths them, tucks the corner.
My father lays the shriveled Christian down.
Three times one week, four times the next. A job
he shares with someone from another church.
He comes home ashen. And every single time,
before he leaves the house he turns to me,
false casually, "You want to come along?"
"Do you need help?" I ask, and he says no.
He leaves. I watch teevee. I'm sixteen, shit!
And I don't want to be a soldier yet.

AT WORK

The white woman steered her loaded cart aside,
out of the checkout lane: "You go ahead."
The drunk black woman snarled, "It's goddamn time
you white folks let us go ahead of you."
She threw her hips into the lane and slammed
a six-pack on the moving belt. Then: *thud!*

The colored woman, like a folding chair,
collapsed. And as she fell, I saw behind her
the stunned white woman holding half
a catsup bottle by the neck. She shrugged.
She looked past me, said "Niggers!," and began
unloading groceries by the register.

When I got home I told my mom. She said,
"I can't keep straight what they want to be called.
I wish they'd make their minds up." Grandmomma knew:
"Oh, negroes, nigras, colored, black — my God!
They're niggers and they know they're niggers too."

When the cops left I'd had to mop it up:
blood, catsup, glass. And since the mop was out,
the boss said hit the produce section too.
So by the time I dumped it down the drain,
the water, without a trace of red, frothed black,
just like it always did. But I enjoyed
slopping the dirty mop across the shoes
of customers who wouldn't move their feet.

THE NEEDS OF THE JOKE TELLER

Jokes always made him nervous. He had to attend to
the perilous needs of the joke-teller.

— Walker Percy

Okay, I got a new one, Sonny said.
Two civil rights protesters block the road,
but, lying there, they get bored and decide
to kill time reading license plates.
"Here come one. It say, Oh aitch eye oh —
Ohio. There's one on your side. What it say?"
"It moving mighty fast, but I makes out
Em eye, ess ess, eye ess ess eye —" Thump! Thump!
And Sonny slapped the table twice and looked up
expectantly, the way joke tellers do.
Dad glared at him, stood, grumbled, left the room.
Mom laughed. Hell, what did I know, I laughed too.
Between silence and laughter, I preferred the mean
uneasy laughter to Daddy's Christian disapproval.
Perhaps you would have made a different choice,
although I've never found that choice
has much to do with laughter. Before math class,
George Hobson turned to me and whispered:
Priest and a rabbi on a train. Priest says,
"I know you're not supposed to eat pork,
but have you ever tried it?" The rabbi
admits he's eaten pork, and he wonders
if perhaps, maybe just once, the priest
had broken vows. The priest confesses,

well, yes, he had slept with a woman.
The rabbi leans back contentedly,
"Better than pork, don't you agree?"
Then George stared in my eyes and leered,
"And man, I tell ya, I love bacon!"
I blushed, and laughed unhappily
till the boy sitting next to me
said, "Don't the pig grease ruin your jeans?"
And then, relieved, I really laughed.
Punch lines are cheerful bullies. They trip
the taboos, knock them to the dirt,
sit on their chests and tickle them
until the unwilling laughter begs,
in tears, for mercy. That's why, at sixteen,
this was my favorite joke:
Young lord goes to a brothel, asks
for the most syphilitic whore
in the establishment. Aghast
— and puzzled — the madam says, *But sir,*
we offer only clean young ladies.
"Well, they won't do. I need the most
infected, suppurating wench
you can provide." *But why, milord?*
"Because I'll go home and I'll tup
the upstairs maid." *You hate the upstairs maid?*
"Oh, good lord, no! I'm fond of her.
But she'll screw the stable boy, who'll hump
the downstairs maid, who'll fuck the groom,

who'll fuck the cook, who'll fuck my father,
and *that's* the bastard that I'm laying for."
I laughed at my own joke. I howled,
stomped, snorted, slapped my thigh,
while my friends laughed uneasily
or didn't laugh at all. I loved
how wicked I felt telling it —
exposed, disloyal. I loved the electric
evasiveness and rage of jokes,
and the suspended moment as the brain
slips on its cogs and freewheels until
the gears catch and the joke becomes
innocuous or horrible — or silly:
To get to the other side. Okay,
you're ugly too. To the dump, to the dump,
to the dump, dump, dump. Loose shoes,
tight pussy, and a warm place to shit.
If the foo shits, wear it. Help find my keys
and — Sam and Janet Evening — we'll drive out
into a memory of me
sitting beneath the kitchen table
piling red blocks on yellow blocks
and knocking them into a heap
while Mother told a friend this joke:
A woman's swimming when a wave
pulls off her top. She crosses her arms
to hide her breasts. Here Mom paused,
looked down at me, and left out the part

about the nipples peeking over
the woman's crossed forearms. A boy
swims to her, dog-paddles, stares
and yells, "Hey, lady, if you're going
to drown those puppies, I want one."
Mom laughed, her laughter throaty, rich, and sheepish.
Each joke's a transgression. But never having seen
a breast or nipple — having seen, at most,
the bulgeless silhouette of Momma's blouse —
I laughed regardless, imagining the joke's
nude woman was my mother, the joke-boy me.
I pictured her stumbling through the waves,
two bobbling puppies rowdy on her chest.
She looked, appraised, and wondered why I laughed.
I laughed to hear my laughter merge with hers.

CHIHUAHUAS

"Don't tell me how to run my house,"
my cousin snarled at her father. *It's not*
your house long's I got money in it,
Sonny snarled right back. They fought about
the eight chihuahuas that stampeded
into her bedroom, hit the wall,
then yip yip yipped down to the kitchen.
They'd skid across linoleum
and pile into *that* wall. Then Midget
and Teeny, Tiny, Itsy, Bitsy,
and Little Bit — you get the drift —
galloped back to the bedroom, where
they'd gnawed one corner off her teevee set.
And Sonny hated them. *Just rats!*
he muttered. He'd turn to me and say,
Your cousin keeps rats in her house,
and worse, she sleeps with them. But not
like Cinderella. She was so huge
she radiated heat, and those
pink dogs huddled against her bulk
until one night — dyspeptic, drunk —
she rolled onto them. Three died. She gave
the living dogs away and found
new things to fuss about with Sonny.
Good stuff, like how she never changed
oil in the old used Dodge he'd bought her,
or scraped the frying pan. I sat
hunch-shouldered at the supper table,

my elbows braced on cracked oilcloth,
and I chose sides. I chose his. Goddamn,
I thought. The poor *are* with you always.
The lazy and the stupid too.
It's just that easy when you're seventeen,
more complicated when you love them
(which then I didn't think I did).
I didn't want to comprehend
her poverty, stupidity,
and hopelessness. I feared compassion
would trap me in a shotgun house,
a day job welding and night work
at Piggly-Wiggly, where I stocked shelves
through most of college. How can I
now turn my back on fear and rage?
They got me out. Well, them and laughter.
I still think those damn dogs are funny.

DANGLING

My daddy cinched a rope around my ankles
and swung me off the roof. Afraid, I dangled
in the second-story apex upside down
and scraped the blistered paint down to raw wood.
He handed down fresh paint. Quick as I could,
I slapped it on the house and every stroke
set me to swinging. Daddy said, Good God,
that it was sloppy work, and he was right
of course. So I was right side up when he
lowered me into the darkness of the well.
I grabbled in black water till I found
the rotting body of a cousin's dog.
I hugged it to my chest and Daddy hauled
the wet, gray rope. I vowed I'd always hate him.
But by the time we reached daylight, the dog
was mostly gone. And by the time I reached
my father's hand, the dog had disappeared.

MOTHER'S FUNERAL

I heaved my thick world history book
above my classmates' heads. It arced,
flapped open, boomed against the blackboard.
Two girls screamed, all the tough boys laughed,
and I felt pretty good until someone,
as always, told. Old Parker let me choose:
five swats or five dull hours copying
from history books. And thus I learned,
in Egypt we'd have painted
a butcher shop on Mother's tomb
so she would not be forced, in death,
to eat her excrement. Instead,
when we looked down the hill we saw
heat shimmer in the Big K parking lot.
And right in front of us we saw
a closed steel casket. Some lost Egyptian myths
exist as openings — and nothing else —
scratched out by punished schoolboys.
And at my desk, pencil in hand,
I wished for a more brutal teacher,
one who had lashed those slack boys till
they'd written all of it, from start
to ever-after. We squirmed on metal chairs
and watched the earnest preacher preach
too long. Grandmomma sulked because
my father hadn't let her choose
the funeral dress. In Egypt, we'd seal
her organs in canopic jars,

except the heart, which stays in place.
We'd pack the corpse with natron, rub
spice, resin, ointment into it.
Inside the linen strips, we'd tuck
gold amulets and scarabs. We sat
on rusty folding chairs — three boys,
one man. I tried to pray for her.
Then I tried not to pray. I wanted
to jump into the hole and shovel,
myself, the damp red chunks of clay.
But the grave was already dug,
and the sides draped with grass-green rugs
as if we didn't know that God,
who exhales life into red clay,
also inhales. And my red-headed mother
would stand in her blue Sunday dress
before the forty-two confessors.
They'd question her and she'd say no
to *eater of the blood, eater of the shadows,*
flame head, breaker of the bones, wry head,
white tooth. The jackal-headed god
would lift her heart and balance it
against the feather, Truth. And then
she'd pass into the afterlife
much like this life but somehow better.
And those of us among the living
turned to a preacher droning on
about the love my mother had

for all of us and all the love
we had for her and it's all true,
each pointless word of it. The priest
dips his right little finger in
an alabaster flask and dabs
the god's brow with the sacred oil,
and, thus sustained, the forces of the holy
lift, for another day, their burdens.
A car door slammed. The preacher droned.
It seems my mother's death was good.
I'm not sure how the logic worked,
though I'm a Christian too. He paused,
and, with a hum, electric motors
lowered the casket. Every fifth day
priests shoulder the god and carry him
through town. They strain to feel his promptings
as he leans left or right, grows heavy,
becomes lighter. Down in the parking lot
a radio blared "Purple Haze."
"Amen," the preacher said. We all
shook hands and talked about the heat.
Nobody talked of Isis gathering
from marsh grass, part by part, the flesh
of scattered Osiris, who isn't real.
But I had not yet read world history.
I talked about the heat, hummed "Purple Haze,"
and tapped the bass line on my thigh.

BICEPS

She tugged her shirtsleeve up, and cocked
her right fist by her ear. “Feel this!”
And when I couldn’t make her biceps budge,
she laughed, pure pleasure. Within two years,
Daddy, in the middle of the night,
lurched through my bedroom door and said,
“Your mother’s passed.” Leukemia.
I forced my arm around his shoulder,
which racked. He stood it for less than a minute
before he staggered down the hall
to tell my brothers. Numb, numb, numb.
I lay there in the darker dark,
and, though I’d known this time was coming, thought,
I should’ve known, I should’ve known.

SEVENTEEN

Ahead of me, the dog reared on its rope,
and swayed. The pickup took a hard left turn,
and the dog tipped off the side. He scrambled, fell,
and scraped along the hot asphalt
before he tumbled back into the air.
I pounded on my horn and yelled. The rope
snapped and the brown dog hurtled into the weeds.
I braked, still pounding on my horn. The truck
stopped too.

We met halfway, and stared
down at the shivering dog, which flinched
and moaned and tried to flick its tail.
Most of one haunch was scraped away
and both hind legs were twisted. *You stupid shit!*
I said. He squinted at me. "Well now, bud —
you best watch what you say to me."
I'd never cussed a grown-up man before.
I nodded. I figured on a beating. He grinned.
"You so damn worried about that ole dog,
he's yours." He strolled back to his truck,
gunned it, and slewed off, spraying gravel.
The dog whined harshly.

By the road,
gnats rose waist-high as I waded through
the dry weeds, looking for a rock.
I knelt down by the dog — tail flick —
and slammed the rock down twice. The first
blow did the job, but I had planned for two.

My hands swept up and down again. I grabbed
the hind legs, swung twice, and heaved the dog
into a clump of butterfly weed and vetch.
But then I didn't know that they had names,
those roadside weeds. His truck was a blue Ford,
the dog a beagle. I was seventeen.
The gnats rose, gathered to one loose cloud,
then scattered through coarse orange and purple weeds.

THE SOCIAL ORDER

"Were any children 'different'?" Mom asked.
I shrugged. She pressed. And I allowed
that one of us was chocolate. Mom laughed,
told Dad, repeated it at church,
and I, first grade, felt stupid and ill used.
From restroom walls I slowly learned
the social order: *All niggers stink*
and *Niggers are the proof that Indians*
fucked buffalo. And finally
things started falling into place:
when Mrs. Johnson's daughter called,
my friend's dad yelled into the phone,
"Ain't no Miz Johnson here. We got
a nigger name of Dorrie works for us."
"Besides," he told us, "I can't keep up.
So far she's been a Patterson,
Jones, Todd, and something else."

At night
I'd kneel down by my bed and pray
the race would breed, like Filipinos,
to the rich brown of breakfast toast,
although I'd never met or seen
a Filipino. But social order
kept me confused. Since early morning
he'd mowed, trimmed hedges, swing-bladed weeds
in her front ditch. "You want some water?"
"Yessum," he said. He drank the water,

and thanked her twice. Aunt Ruth smiled,
set the jar gently in the sink,
and after he'd gone back to work,
she shattered it with a claw hammer.
Maybe you know what to say.
I don't. I love some of these people.
Let Jesus love them all. Let Jesus
love every fucking one of us.

HUGE

In the restroom, I sat and strained
and read the walls — *I really need*
a blow job — and somehow I knew
not to ask Momma what that meant.
I stared and turned away and then
turned back to the hairy scrotum suspended
from the huge disembodied cock
drawn on the toilet door. It scared me.
But what's a blow job? Not till high school
did I get an answer: Near downtown
a priest gets off a bus. A whore calls,
"For ten bucks I'll give you a blow job."
"No thanks," he says, not knowing what
a blow job is. Like me. Naive.
He walks two blocks and passes another whore,
who whispers, "Psst, Padre. Ten bucks for a blow job."
"No, ma'am." Like me, the priest is shy
and more polite the more perplexed
he gets. Back at the monastery,
he asks the abbot, "What's a blow job?"
And the abbot — all together now —
says, "Ten bucks, same as downtown."
For days I'd planned exactly how
to ask my question: "Momma, do we
have babies like dogs do?" "Huh?"
She looked unhappy. "You know, the boy
dog flopping on the girl dog's back."
Next day she handed me a book

by a Jesuit who railed against
touching yourself down there, and since
I'd never touched myself down there
except to pee, I stood before the toilet,
jerked once, jerked twice and three times — ouch!
Too young. But once I discovered how
to enrapture the flesh by deceiving it,
I couldn't stop myself. To think
of doing something was the same
as doing it, the Bible says,
though many theologians wish Saint Paul
had only thought that verse. At night,
sweating, the flames of hellfire crackling
beneath my mattress and box spring,
I argued with Saint Paul. He lost.
I couldn't sleep face down: it bent;
and, face up, the sheet sagged on its tent pole.
When I got up to pee, it slapped
my belly. It boing boing boinged
like the curb feeler on my uncle's Dodge,
and I, like Onan, spilt my seed,
simply so I could go to sleep.

As soon as George began fourth grade,
I went to his room, shut the door,
and told him all the fundamentals,
then asked, "Do you have any questions?"
No, Georgie didn't have a question.

He understood it all. I paused,
hand on the doorknob. "Anytime
you want to talk, just let me know,
okay? You don't have to ask Daddy."
I turned the knob. "Well, maybe I have
one question," George said. "What's a vagina?"
Good question, Georgie! I'm glad you asked.
It's something I'd wondered about myself.
I'd seen it on the toilet walls,
and there the hairy black cleft looked
as scary as the penises,
as huge. When we passed girls with streaked hair,
short skirts, high heels, tight blouses, and just
a little wiggle in their walk,
Mom said, "Those are the kind of girls
who get young boys in trouble." How, Momma?
"You just stay away from them and you
won't ever have to know." Thanks, Mom.
Which left me locked inside my body,
which I explored though it was small,
not huge. And from my body flew
white spunk and yellow rivers. Eros
and Thanatos, both coming and going.

"Let's tell of our first time," she said,
our hostess. She'd been drinking. "Let's not,"
I said. But with a few more drinks,
folks launched into their back-seat stories,
and when my turn turned up, I said,

abashed, "Well, on my wedding night . . ."
They laughed. They thought I was joking,
which is my custom. But now I'm angry
because I'm laughing at these things.
When I was living them, I vowed
I'd never give them over to cheap humor.
Well, what else do you want to do,
serious boy? Cry? Yes, cry.
And fight and scream a little too.
But for the moment this uneasy
careering back and forth across
the serious and not-so-serious
gives me a way of saying what
should be but cannot yet be said,
if ever. When I was six, I loved
my stutter. My parents dreaded it,
which made me love it even more.
I loved the words' resistance, loved
how the *puh, puh, puh* spun on my lips
as if it didn't want to leave my body
and take place in the world of men
and women. But now it does, and much
of what I thought I'd never say
I've written down, laughed at, and kept
against forgetting, which I had longed for.

BURIAL INSURANCE

It came each month from Omaha
and Mother tossed it on my bed.
"This is for you." But what it was
I had a hard time figuring —
short articles on Arbor Day,
patriotism, and my insurance needs:
The Woodman Magazine. I asked,
but never got much of an answer.
The last page printed dumb "Woodchuckles,"
from which I learned a favorite poem,
my first: "Big Ole had a goat.
The goat had halitosis. And everywhere
Big Ole went, the people held
their noses." And now a literary critic,
I realize it's not a whole poem,
but just the start of one. I want
to know much more about this man
and his relationship with his goat,
and both of theirs to a society
that spurns their gifts. But I digress.
The point is, I accepted everything,
interpreted nothing. I couldn't know
that every time my mother tossed
that magazine in my direction,
she thought — I am interpreting —
of my dead sister, secret Andrea,
dead one short year before my birth
and never talked about at all,

and how the first thing bought for me
was burial insurance. My sister:
car wreck, a patch of ice near Dothan.
That's the story Grandmomma told.
Although I've been much unemployed
and worse, a poet, in Daddy's eyes
I'm still some version of success:
I'm forty years old, I'm alive.
Sometimes that's all it comes down to.
And through me, I am proud to say,
live Ole, his goat, and its bad breath.
Why did the goat's breath smell so bad?
Did Ole's wife dislike the goat?
Or was the goat a consolation
to Ole after his wife died?
But this is not a Chekhov story.
I was my parents' consolation —
something to fear for, hover over,
resist loving too much. Grandmomma said
my sister's dying was God's punishment,
they thought, for loving her too much,
for sin, for making her an idol
before the Lord. Interpretation.
I'll gloss this story with another.
A white rat, stepped on by my brother,
raced madly in tight clockwise circles
for two days; then it died. For me,
that did it. No more pets. And that

was for a rat. Before my birth
they took care of my death. Once burned.
I get the statement twice a year.
It asks, "Have you insured your lifestyle?"
Although I'd much prefer to end
with Ole and his goat's bad breath,
which seems to me — interpretation —
to represent mortality, I'm forced
to come back to my sister Andrea.
What did it cost to bury her?
I don't mean emotionally. I mean
in dollars on the barrelhead
and how long they worked to pay it off.
My policy is eight hundred dollars.
Sometimes that's what it comes down to.
But finally things do end with Ole,
who lives eternally because
he never lived. I know him better
than I know Andrea because I'm free
to speculate, invent, and ask about
the man, the goat, its halitosis.
Andrea. Each time we visited,
Grandmomma took her picture off the wall.

HUNTING WITH MY BROTHER

My brother blasts pigeons beneath the bridge
and lets them lie. *They're only flying rats,*
he says, and just like Daddy I snap, "Two wrongs
don't make a right." *But two rights make a left,*
he says. We laugh, and talk of how his wife
cooks squirrels with dumplings and black pepper
and how my garden's gone to seed.

He swings the shotgun to his shoulder. Two quick
squirrels scrabble, spiraling up a water oak.
Frustrated, Jack fires into the ragged nests.
"Hey, knock it off," I yell. He shrugs,
twists up the choke, and fires again.
I grab the barrel and wrench it. His fist
clips my left ear. I cock my fist,
but we're already backing off,
apologizing.
                    We hike two miles in silence.
Jack's wife looks from the kitchen window.
We hold up empty hands and shrug. She laughs.
We glare at her and, goddamn, she laughs louder.
Then slowly we laugh too. Who wouldn't laugh
at Cain and Abel coming home —
no meat, no beans, and both alive.

AFTERWORD

As a child, I swore I'd tell my story
while I was still angry,
even if mine were just the rage,
as Mother argued, of a high-strung boy,
unkind and oversensitive.
Now, having told my story, said my piece,
I'm not as angry as I was,
but tired. And guilty. All telling's betrayal,
I've learned again: selection, rounding off,
interpretation and my failure
to stay as angry as I'd vowed.

One night, after I'd read from these poems,
somebody earnest came up to me and asked,
"How can you forgive your family?"
"By asking them to forgive me,"
I said, pleased with myself for being
so facile under pressure. But now
I think I may have got it right.
Each week when I call Daddy on the phone,
we talk about the weather, politics,
church, football, grandkids — and then we struggle
to say *I love you,* although it's true and gets
a little truer with each saying,
and less complex. Every time we moved,
we scrubbed the old house clean,
then scoured the new one. Abrasives, bleach,
and toothpicks for the crevices.
And if, despite our scrubbing, dirt remained,
Mom said, "It's our dirt now. It's clean."